LET'S CELEBRATE CHRISTMAS

by Peter and Connie Roop

Illustrated by
Katy Keck Arnsteen

The Millbrook Press
Brookfield, Connecticut

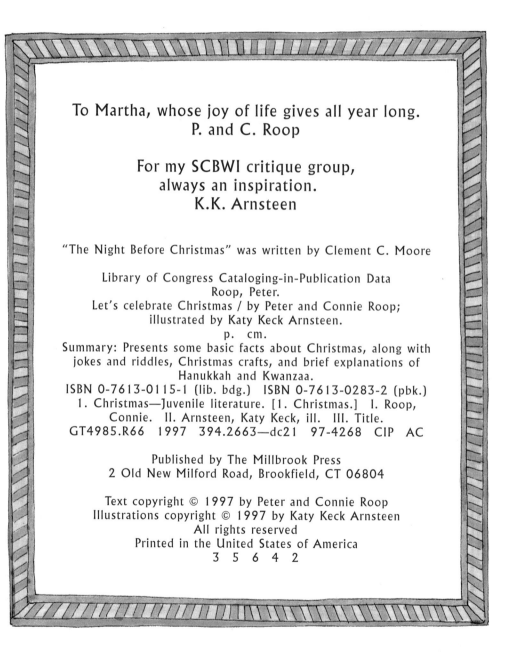

To Martha, whose joy of life gives all year long.
P. and C. Roop

For my SCBWI critique group,
always an inspiration.
K.K. Arnsteen

"The Night Before Christmas" was written by Clement C. Moore

Library of Congress Cataloging-in-Publication Data
Roop, Peter.
Let's celebrate Christmas / by Peter and Connie Roop;
illustrated by Katy Keck Arnsteen.
p. cm.
Summary: Presents some basic facts about Christmas, along with
jokes and riddles, Christmas crafts, and brief explanations of
Hanukkah and Kwanzaa.
ISBN 0-7613-0115-1 (lib. bdg.) ISBN 0-7613-0283-2 (pbk.)
1. Christmas—Juvenile literature. [1. Christmas.] I. Roop,
Connie. II. Arnsteen, Katy Keck, ill. III. Title.
GT4985.R66 1997 394.2663—dc21 97-4268 CIP AC

Published by The Millbrook Press
2 Old New Milford Road, Brookfield, CT 06804

Mexico
Feliz Navidad

France
Joyeux Noël

Italy
Buon Natale

China
Kung Hsi
Hsin Nien

Poland
Wesolych Swiat

MERRY CHRISTMAS from AROUND THE WORLD!

Germany
Fröhliche
Weihnachten

Japan
Meri Kurisumasu

Ethiopia
Melkm Ganna

South Africa
Een Plesierige
Kerfees

Sweden
Glad Jul

Brazil
Boas Festas

Holland
Gelukkig
Kerstfeest

WHY DO WE CELEBRATE CHRISTMAS?

Christmas Day is observed by Christians to celebrate the birth of Jesus. No one knows the exact day he was born, but in the year 349 Pope Julius I chose December 25 to be Jesus' birthday.

There was a good reason for this choice. Many festivals were already being held around this time to honor other gods. By linking Jesus' birth to these celebrations, the pope hoped people would also honor Jesus and become Christians.

One celebration was the Birthday of the Unconquered Sun. Because the winter sun wasn't as warm, and the days were shorter, people built huge fires on hills and mountaintops to give the sun strength. Although we no longer burn fires on hilltops, lights are everywhere at Christmastime—on trees, in windows, and decorating city streets.

Who hangs around your house at Christmas?

Holly!

What song does a monkey sing at Christmas?

Jungle Bells!

What king do you see every Christmas?

A stock-king!

What do we have on Christmas Day that we don't have any other day of the year?

Christmas!

Knock, knock!
Who's there?
Mary.
Mary who?
Mary Christmas!

WHO IS SANTA CLAUS?

Santa Claus was a real person named Nicholas. Nicholas was a Christian bishop who lived in Asia Minor long ago. Nicholas especially enjoyed giving treats to poor children. He helped so many needy and poor people that the Catholic Church made him a saint. Feasts were given to honor Saint Nicholas's birthday on December 6. Parents told their children Saint Nicholas would give them presents if they were good.

In Holland, Dutch children put out their wooden shoes, hoping Saint Nick would fill them with candy and treats. They called him Sinter Klaas. Sinter Klaas did not come in a sleigh but in a ship! Then he rode a white horse as he went from home to home. Children put out carrots, water, and hay for Sinter Klaas's horse. Sinter Klaas became our Santa Claus when many Dutch people settled in America.

Santa is called Grandfather Frost in Russia. Presents are brought on Christmas Eve by an old woman named Babouschka.

In Japan, Santa is called Hoteiosho. He has eyes in the back of his head to watch for good children. He gives gifts out of his pack.

In Sweden children wait for Jultomten at Christmas.

WHY DOES SANTA COME DOWN THE CHIMNEY?

People long ago believed in a goddess named Hertha.
Hertha watched over their homes. She protected them from illness.
As winter began, families had a special feast to honor Hertha. They
built huge fires in their fireplaces. Hertha
would come down the chimney through the smoke to
give them good luck for the next year. Our word
"hearth" comes from Hertha.

These early beliefs about Hertha are thought to be the
reason why we believe our Santa Claus comes down the chimney.
Santa, however, doesn't bring us good luck. Instead he brings us
presents for being good the past year. Even
if you don't have a chimney, Santa will find you if
you have been good.

In Sweden, Jultomten arrives in a sleigh pulled by a goat.

In Mexico, the Three Kings bring gifts and the children leave straw out for the kings' camels.

In Ghana, the children believe that Father Christmas comes from the jungle.

In a part of Australia, a white-bearded Santa wearing a red bathing suit arrives on water skis.

In China, Lan Khoong-Khoong (Nice Old Father) brings presents to children's stockings.

WHY DO WE GIVE PRESENTS AT CHRISTMAS?

Gift-giving in December is an old custom. At the ancient December festivals people gave gifts of candles, lamps, and evergreens to their friends and families. Others gave money to help the poor.

In the Bible story, Joseph and Mary go to an inn but there is no room for them. They are sent to the stable, and that night Jesus is born. He is laid in a manger with animals all around. Overhead a bright star shines, showing the way to the Three Kings who come to see the new baby, bringing precious gifts of gold, frankincense, and myrrh. Myrrh and frankincense are sweet-smelling gums used in perfumes. Gold meant that someday Jesus would be a king. Frankincense meant he would be a high priest. Myrrh, also used in embalming, foretold his death.

SAINT NICHOLAS' DAY
DECEMBER 6

People in
Belgium and
Holland exchange
gifts on this day.

SAINT STEPHEN'S DAY
DECEMBER 26

This is also known
as Boxing Day
in England,
because of all the
Christmas boxes.

ST. LUCIA'S DAY
DECEMBER 13

This is the
gift-giving day
in Sweden.

EPIPHANY
JANUARY 6

Many Catholic
countries give
gifts to celebrate
the Epiphany.

WHY DO WE HANG STOCKINGS AT CHRISTMAS?

A special Christmas tradition is hanging your stocking for Santa to fill with small presents. This tradition comes to us from Holland, where children hang stockings for Sinter Klaas to fill.

But why stockings? Here is one story. Long ago there was a merchant who had three daughters. Sadly, the merchant somehow lost all of his money. His daughters were going to be sold as servants to pay his bills. During their last night at home the girls washed their stockings and hung them by the fire to dry. Bishop Nicholas, hearing about their fate, dropped gold down the chimney into each girl's stocking. The girls were saved! When their father heard who had given the gold, he went around town praising Bishop Nicholas.

Ever since, children have hung stockings by the chimney in the hopes that Santa Claus will fill their stockings with gifts, too.

WHAT IS A CRÈCHE?

A crèche is a manger scene showing Mary,
Joseph, and the baby Jesus. Most often the animals
who would have been in the stable are also shown.
The scene was first created in 1224 by Saint
Francis in Italy. He used real people and animals.
Today we have wooden or plastic people and
animals to re-create the Nativity scene.

WHY DO WE DECORATE TREES?

Legend has it that a German man named Martin
Luther went walking in the woods on a starry Christmas Eve.
Starlight twinkled on the snowy branches of the fir trees.
Martin Luther cut down a fir tree, took it home, and decorated
it with candles so that it twinkled like the sparkling trees
in the forest. People enjoyed his tree so much,
they wanted one for themselves.

The first Christmas trees were small—often just
the tops of taller trees. The idea of bringing in a tall tree
stretching from floor to ceiling began later in America.

The first decorations were apples, paper roses,
cookies, candy, and candles. Later, nuts, gingerbread,
toys, dolls, oranges, glass icicles, and balls and
other ornaments were added.

Not all trees were decorated with expensive
ornaments. Many pioneer children decorated their trees
with pinecones, seed pods, strings of popcorn and
cranberries, and other natural ornaments. Farm children
often made gingerbread ornaments in the shapes of
animals. Fat hogs, hopping rabbits, and galloping
horses hung on many family Christmas trees.

A star is often placed at the top of the Christmas tree.
This star represents the star shining over Bethlehem when Jesus
was born. Some families place paper or glass
angels on their treetops.

Early Christmas trees were beautiful with their
ornaments and glittering candles. But having lighted candles
on a tree was dangerous. The tree might catch fire. About
a hundred years ago Thomas Edison invented the electric
lightbulb. One of his friends put some of Edison's lights on his
Christmas tree. With electric lights people could enjoy a
lighted Christmas tree and worry less about fire. Since
then, trees inside and outside have been
shining brilliantly at Christmastime.

President Teddy Roosevelt did not want people cutting down trees, so he did not allow a Christmas tree in the White House. His two sons, however, smuggled a tree into their closet.

The General Grant Tree in California is our national Christmas Tree. This giant sequoia is 267 feet tall and is over 3,500 years old.

Old Christmas trees are used for lining snowmobile paths, sunk in lakes to make homes for fish, or ground up to make chips for hiking trails.

Christmas trees are grown in all fifty states, including Hawaii!

WHY DO WE SING CAROLS AT CHRISTMAS?

The first Christmas carols were dance tunes, not Christmas songs. Long ago in Greece, a "carol" was a ring of dancers who danced to flute music. The men and women dancers formed a chain holding hands as they danced.

Carol dancing was such fun that it became part of many Christmas festivities. In many Spanish-speaking countries, dancing and singing are a Christmas highlight.

Christmas music is a wonderful part of the season. Many popular carols, like "Silent Night" and "Hark! The Herald Angels Sing," came from Europe. "O Little Town of Bethlehem" and "We Three Kings of Orient Are" were written in America especially for children.

In America, going from house to house singing carols is popular. Swedish children sing carols and dance with their parents around the family Christmas tree. In France carols are often sung during Christmas plays and pageants. In Wales many carols are sung to gentle music of a harp. In Puerto Rico, carolers ride on horseback, singing their songs to music of guitars and maracas. All around the world, music is a special part of the Christmas season.

WHAT KINDS OF FOOD DO PEOPLE EAT ON CHRISTMAS?

Most families have traditional dishes that they like to serve every year. Some of the dishes described on this page are only made for Christmas because they are richer and more difficult to make.

Bûche de Noël is a rich chocolate cake from France made to look like a Yule log.

In Sweden they make pepparkakor—Christmas gingersnaps.

Plum pudding from England contains no plums and is not a pudding but a delicious cake.

Stollen and Lebkuchen are treats from Germany studded with candied fruits.

In England the Christmas dinner table is set with crackers, hollow paper tubes filled with candies or small goodies.

Christmas cookies in America are shaped like trees and wreaths and are often made and decorated by the whole family.

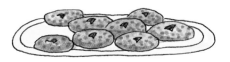

Kourabiedes from Greece are cookies that each have a clove, to symbolize the spices brought to Jesus by the Three Kings.

Panettone is a sweet raisin and chestnut-studded holiday bread from Italy.

Gingerbread has been a holiday treat since the 14th century. It is used to make gingerbread men and enchanting gingerbread houses.

DO SOME OF YOUR FRIENDS CELEBRATE HANUKKAH?

Long ago Jewish people held a special festival in December that continues today. This celebration is called Hanukkah, or the Feast of Lights. Hanukkah is celebrated in honor of the Lord saving the Jews from their enemies.

Hanukkah lasts for eight days. A candlestick called a menorah is put in a special place in the home. Each day a new candle is lit until all eight are burning brightly. Gifts wrapped in blue and white paper are exchanged. Fried potato pancakes called latkes are served with sour cream and applesauce. Playing games is a fun part of Hanukkah. One game is spinning the dreidel, a four-sided top. Each side has a letter on it. You win candy or coins or nothing depending on which letter lands up.

Make a Menorah Banner

Materials: Four pieces of 9 x 12 in. felt
(1 white, 1 yellow, 2 blue)
glue
scissors
ruler

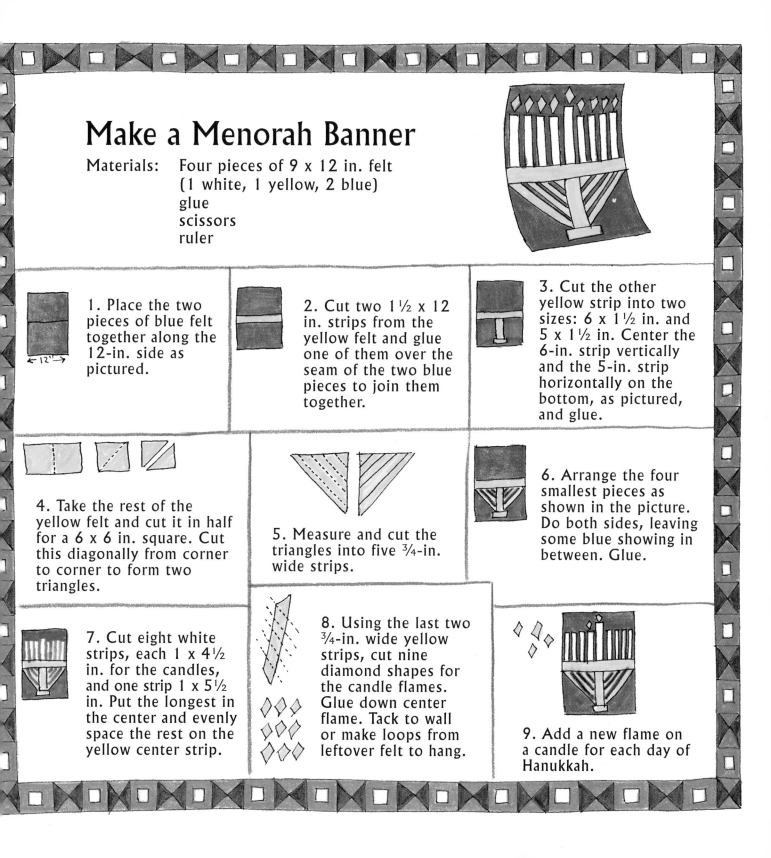

1. Place the two pieces of blue felt together along the 12-in. side as pictured.

← 12″ →

2. Cut two 1½ x 12 in. strips from the yellow felt and glue one of them over the seam of the two blue pieces to join them together.

3. Cut the other yellow strip into two sizes: 6 x 1½ in. and 5 x 1½ in. Center the 6-in. strip vertically and the 5-in. strip horizontally on the bottom, as pictured, and glue.

4. Take the rest of the yellow felt and cut it in half for a 6 x 6 in. square. Cut this diagonally from corner to corner to form two triangles.

5. Measure and cut the triangles into five ¾-in. wide strips.

6. Arrange the four smallest pieces as shown in the picture. Do both sides, leaving some blue showing in between. Glue.

7. Cut eight white strips, each 1 x 4½ in. for the candles, and one strip 1 x 5½ in. Put the longest in the center and evenly space the rest on the yellow center strip.

8. Using the last two ¾-in. wide yellow strips, cut nine diamond shapes for the candle flames. Glue down center flame. Tack to wall or make loops from leftover felt to hang.

9. Add a new flame on a candle for each day of Hanukkah.

DO SOME OF YOUR FRIENDS CELEBRATE KWANZAA?

Kwanzaa is a special African-American celebration that lasts seven days. Kwanzaa begins on December 26 and runs through January 1. Kwanzaa is rooted in African harvest festivals called First Fruits. These harvest celebrations have been shared throughout Africa for hundreds of years. The days for Kwanzaa match the times First Fruits are celebrated in Africa.

There are seven principles honored during Kwanzaa, each highlighted with its own candle in a kinara, or candleholder. Each day a new principle is celebrated and a new candle lit.

The principles are Umoja (unity), Kujichagulia (self-determination), Ujima (working together and responsibility), Ujamaa (cooperative economics), Nia (purpose), Kuumba (creativity), and Imani (faith). During Kwanzaa, families come together, gifts are shared, and thanks are given.

Dr. Maulana Karenga created Kwanzaa in 1966 for African Americans to honor their ancestors and their traditions.

MAKE A MKEKA, THE KWANZAA PLACEMAT

Here is what you need:

large sheets of red, black, and green construction paper,
scissors, glue, and a ruler.

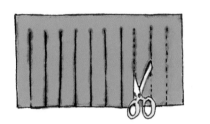

1. Measure 1 in. down from the long edge of your paper. Then cut 1-in. strips vertically to that line.

2. Cut the other 2 pieces of paper into 1-in. strips the long way.

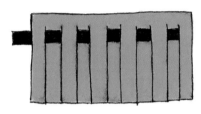

3. Weave one strip under and over the vertical cuts until you get to the end.

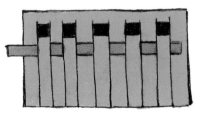

4. Weave the second strip of a different color by going over and under.

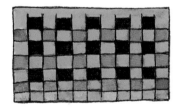

5. Continue weaving until you run out of room. Glue the ends down so they will not slip out.

6. You can glue a card to the back of your placemat explaining the colors: Red is for the struggle to be free, black is for unity, and green is for a better future.

IT IS JUST AS NICE TO GIVE
AS IT IS TO RECEIVE!

Some of the best gifts are the ones you make yourself!

OLD-FASHIONED CLOVED FRUIT. You will need: Oranges and lemons, cloves, thimble. Push the slender end of the cloves into the fruit in a pretty pattern. You don't have to cover the whole fruit, although you could. Put a thimble on your thumb to help push the cloves in. Pin a loop of ribbon to the top of the fruit so it can hang, or put two or three decorated fruits in a bowl.

PICTURE ORNAMENT. You will need: Christmas card or your drawing of a Christmas tree, pictures of yourself and your family, cardboard, string. Draw a Christmas tree, or cut one out of an old Christmas card. Carefully cut out round spaces to look like ornaments and tape pictures of yourself and your family so your faces show through the holes. Glue the tree onto a cardboard backing. Tape a string onto the frame, and friends and family can enjoy you hanging around every Christmas!

PINECONE BIRD FEEDER. You will need: Pinecone, yarn, peanut butter, birdseed. Take a pinecone and tie a piece of strong yarn around the base. Cover the pinecone with peanut butter. Roll the pinecone in birdseed and hang it from a branch outside. You can put more peanut butter and seeds on the cone when the birds have finished. Try different seeds to see what they like.

BARRETTE HOLDER. You will need: Yarn, ribbon, glue. Make a thick 12-in. braid of different-colored pieces of yarn. Decorate with a ribbon bow on the top and bottom. Attach a loop to the top.

NO-MESS MESSAGE BOARD. You will need: Cardboard, big colored rubber bands, 24-in. string, glue. Cut four pieces of cardboard, each measuring 9 x 9 in. Glue the first two pieces together and then glue the other two pieces together. Now position the string so that 3 in. on both ends are on the cardboard. Glue the two double pieces of cardboard together with the string in between. When the glue has dried, cover the board with crisscrossing rubber bands. Keep adding rubber bands until you are happy with the way it looks. Use at least ten rubber bands. Decorate with stickers or leave it plain. Tuck a new pencil and some scrap paper under a rubber band.

MAKE A CHRISTMAS GARLAND

There are lots of different kinds of garlands you can make, and lots of places to put them. Think about decorating the Christmas tree, doorways, and mantlepieces.

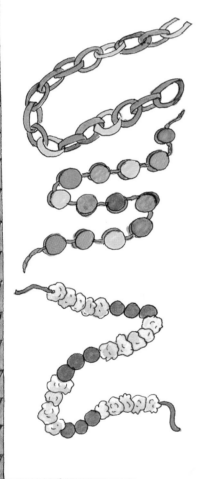

CHRISTMAS RINGS: Cut colored construction paper into strips 1/2 in. to 1 in. wide. With your first strip tape the ends together to make a ring. Take the second strip and run it through the first ring before taping the ends together. You can make all the rings the same size, or you can make them all different sizes, or try one big ring then one small, etc.

CIRCLE STRINGS: Cut a long piece of yarn. Then cut out 1-in. circles from colored papers. Paste two circles together with the yarn centered in between, and as you paste try to leave the same amount of yarn between the circles. Decorate the circles with glued-on glitter, felt pens, or tin foil.

POPCORN AND CRANBERRY ROPE: Thread a long sturdy needle with heavy-duty thread. Run the needle through five or six pieces of popcorn and then two or three cranberries. Leave plenty of thread at each end because you will have to tie your rope together to make one long garland. This garland can go outside to wish the birds a Merry Christmas!

WRAP IT UP!

Make your own wrapping paper!

The funny papers make great wrapping paper. Finish it off with brightly colored yarn or ribbon.

Open up a grocery bag so that it lies flat. Decorate with pictures from old Christmas cards, glitter, felt-tipped pens, glued swirls of yarn, or wrapped hard candies, glued on. Or leave the paper plain and top off your package with small pine branches knotted in the ribbon.

Small lunch bags or bakery bags are perfect for odd-shaped presents. Decorate the bag with some of the ideas described above. Punch holes along the top and weave in ribbon or yarn for a drawstring.

THE NIGHT BEFORE CHRISTMAS

'Twas the night before Christmas, when all through the house,
Not a creature was stirring, not even a mouse.
The stockings were hung by the chimney with care,
In hopes that St. Nicholas soon would be there.
The children were nestled all snug in their beds,
While visions of sugarplums danced in their heads.
And Mama in her kerchief and I in my cap
Had just settled our brains for a long winter's nap.
When out on the lawn there arose such a clatter,
I sprang from my bed to see what was the matter.
Away to the window I flew like a flash,
Tore open the shutters and threw up the sash.
The moon on the breast of the new-fallen snow
Gave the luster of midday to objects below.
When, what to my wondering eyes should appear,
But a miniature sleigh, and eight tiny reindeer.
With a little old driver, so lively and quick,
I knew in a moment it must be St. Nick.
More rapid than eagles his coursers they came,
And he whistled, and shouted, and called them by name:
"Now, Dasher! Now, Dancer! Now, Prancer and Vixen!
On, Comet! On, Cupid! On, Donder and Blitzen!
To the top of the porch, to the top of the wall!
Now dash away, dash away, dash away all!"
As dry leaves that before the wild hurricane fly,
When they meet with an obstacle, mount to the sky.

So up to the housetop the coursers they flew,
With a sleigh full of toys, and St. Nicholas, too!
And then in a twinkling, I heard on the roof,
The prancing and pawing of each little hoof.
As I drew in my head, and was turning around,
Down the chimney St. Nicholas came with a bound.
He was dressed all in fur, from his head to his foot,
And his clothes were all tarnished with ashes and soot.
A bundle of toys he had flung on his back,
And he looked like a peddler just opening his pack.
His eyes how they twinkled! His dimples how merry!
His cheeks were like roses, his nose like a cherry.
His droll little mouth was drawn up like a bow,
And the beard on his chin was as white as the snow.
The stump of a pipe he held tight in his teeth,
And the smoke, it encircled his head like a wreath.
He had a broad face and a little round belly
That shook, when he laughed, like a bowl full of jelly.
He was chubby and plump, a right jolly old elf,
And I laughed when I saw him in spite of myself.
A wink of his eye, and a twist of his head,
Soon gave me to know I had nothing to dread.
He spoke not a word, but went straight to his work,
And filled all the stockings, then turned with a jerk.
And laying his finger aside of his nose,
And giving a nod, up the chimney he rose.
He sprang to his sleigh, to his team gave a whistle,
And away they all flew like the down of a thistle.
But I heard him exclaim, ere he drove out of sight,
"HAPPY CHRISTMAS TO ALL, AND TO ALL A GOOD NIGHT!"

ABOUT THE AUTHORS

Connie and Peter Roop have been making and giving presents all their lives. Both are teachers who share the gift of their knowledge with children every day of the year. The authors of twenty-five books, they also share their love of reading and writing with children across America. They are the parents of Sterling and Heidi, who share their gifts of love and friendship around Appleton, Wisconsin, and in the many places to which the Roop family travels.

ABOUT THE ILLUSTRATOR

Katy Keck Arnsteen has illustrated over forty books for children. Her background in fine arts and teaching combines for bright illustrations.